Sally MacColl has spent her whole life on the beautiful Hebridean island of Mull, where she is co-owner of the Tobermory Fish Company, her family-owned business since 1971.

Bob Dewar has illustrated over 40 books, including all of Birlinn's acclaimed Food Bibles, and his work has featured in the *Scotman*, *Herald*, *Sunday Post* and *Scottish Field*.

The *Tobermory Seafood* Bible

Sally MacColl

Introduction by Gary Maclean

Illustrated by Bob Dewar

BIRLINN

First published in 2021 by
Birlinn Limited
West Newington House
10 Newington Road
Edinburgh
EH9 1QS

www.birlinn.co.uk

ISBN: 978 1 78027 754 7

British Library Cataloguing-in-Publication Data
A catalogue record for this book is available from
the British Library

Designed and typeset by Mark Blackadder

Printed and bound by Bell & Bain Ltd, Glasgow

Contents

Quick and Easy Ways with Smoked Fish

Quick and Easy Ways to Prepare and Cook Shellfish

Our Favourite Fish Recipes

Sides and Sauces

Foreword

I was delighted and honoured when I was asked by Sally to write the foreword for this amazing book. This is an incredible collection of recipes using some of Scotland's most stunning products.

From a very young age I have always been fascinated by the Isle of Mull. Being a Maclean and Mull being the ancient ancestral home of the Macleans, it is a place I have always wanted to visit and get to know better. As chefs, we are well aware of the standard of produce that comes from Mull. I fell in love with the food of Mull long before I ever got the chance to visit and work there. For a small island, the food producers there punch well above their weight in the food world. None more so than the Tobermory Fish Company.

The first time I visited the Tobermory Fish Company and met Sally was when I was filming a show for the BBC called *Landward*. I was presenting a segment of the show that followed me learning all about my favourite Scottish ingredients, so I decided to get over to Mull and meet the people who are at the forefront of the amazing food the island provides.

I was lucky to be able to spend time with Sally and her mum, who gave me a crash course in everything that they do. I was totally captivated with the place, and more importantly the food they produced was simply amazing. I learned loads about not only the smokehouse but the way Sally embraces food and products from the whole island. Since then we have kept in touch and I have followed her journey with food. She is a wonderful ambassador for Scottish fish and shellfish; this book is a fantastic collection of her knowledge, and I am so happy she has put pen to paper and shared these beautiful recipes with us all.

Gary Maclean

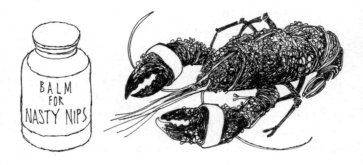

Introduction

When you're young and growing up, you don't really give much thought to where you live. It just seemed normal to play around brightly coloured houses, walk on beaches and swim in a crystal-clear sea. Without a second thought I would go out in a boat with family and friends. Leaving the bay we'd head north. Out past the Rubha nan Gall lighthouse and, turning west, we'd look up the cliffs at the spectacular Glengorm Castle, where I worked for four happy years with Tom and Marjorie Nelson. After a while, excitment would take over and my brother, Douglas, and I couldn't wait to drop in a couple of fishing lines to see if we could catch a really big fish, a 'lunker', in my dad's words. On the boat you are always on the lookout for dolphins, porpoises and whales. Often we would pass a basking shark lazily swimming on the surface as we headed towards Calgary Bay. Soon the anchor would go down and, after a short row to shore, the barbecue was set up on the white sands for a feast of fish and shellfish. Just before sunset every-one would climb the hill beside the beach and watch the sun dip down behind the Isle of Coll on the horizon. It was only as I grew older that I came to realise that where I lived was really special.

In 1788 the British Society for Encouraging Fisheries decided to build a port – to quote their words, 'upon a wonderful natural harbour among seas of abundant fish and shellfish of outstanding quality'. The name of that port, and my home town, is Tobermory, on the Hebridean Isle of Mull. My work-place is at a company started in 1971 by my grandparents, called the Tobermory Fish Company. The smokehouse and shop is situated just above Tobermory Bay at Baliscate. On Mull you can't get away from history. Above our smokehouse and amongst the trees are the tumbled remains of a Celtic Christian chapel from the seventh century. I often wonder who walked up the hill path, past our smokehouse, carrying fish and seafoods all those generations ago. I work alongside my mum. She is an absolute hero. As head of production it's her job to make sure everything that comes out of our smoker is perfection. And I can tell you she won't settle for anything less.

My passion for food started when I worked at Glengorm Castle as a teenager. I found that a question I was getting asked all the time was 'Where can I buy some of your delicious local seafood?' And that question was completely justified for, unless you knew the fisherman, there really wasn't an outlet for visitors to purchase and take home some of the amazing foods from our Hebridean seas.

One day I spoke to my mum and dad. What about refurbishing my grandparents' company with a fully fitted-out retail shop selling local seafoods and produce? It didn't actually take much to convince them it was a good idea. That was it settled. We were going ahead. After a year's tough renovation, dusting off Grandpa's recipe book and Mum retraining herself on how to use the smoker, all was ready. In February 2011 the company opened again for business and it's been non-stop ever since.

It always amazing to me that such long a time has now passed since my grandparents opened the doors and we are all still really enjoying every day at the Tobermory Fish Company. I work beside my mum and dad and it's such a treat. We seem to work very well together as a team and are always looking at adapting and growing the business where we can, while still keeping it a very intimate, fun and happy place to work.

It really is a family affair with my husband Scott and twin brother Douglas helping out when they can but also pursuing careers in engineering.

Christmas is a brilliant time as we get to contact our family of mail order customers. Many are still with us from when my grandparents started the business. We have become like personal friends over the years. Family are also a great help in December when the Christmas orders start coming in. Every year we have no idea how it's going to go, but we have been lucky so far as each year has got busier and busier. Starts can be at 6am and Mum often has to work through the night until we have sent out our all the packs and gift boxes to customers all over the country.

We have families who have been eating Tobermory trout as a Christmas tradition for generations. Often their grandparents were on our early mailing lists from back when my grandparents started all those years ago. Their custom has been passed on through the years just as the business has been passed down to me. It fills me with so much joy to know that our produce connects them to their parents and grandparents just as the business has done in my case.

Health and Seafood

In today's world of ready meals and snacking, the value of healthy eating has never been more important. Not only are fish and shellfish delicious, they are also two of the healthiest things you can put on your plate. Fish is great for your heart, it improves circulation, keeps your joints mobile, your eyes bright and contains essential minerals. There's even evidence that you could get a boost in brain power from it! We should all aim to eat at least two portions of seafood every week.

One thing I'm often asked is which seafood is best for you? The great news is all seafood is good for you. White fish such as cod, halibut and haddock are excellent sources of protein and low in fat. The more 'oily' fish such as salmon, trout and mackerel have high levels of Omega-3 fatty acids. Shellfish are also important for a healthy diet with high levels of protein, low levels of fats and lots of essential minerals such as zinc, which boosts the immune system.

If I'm freezing fish or shellfish I do it at once by

marking the date clearly on the pack, to use within ten months. I never re-freeze thawed raw seafoods. Granny's old adage is always running through my mind – 'if in doubt, throw it out'.

When preparing fish or shellfish, cross-contamination is a very real risk. I always wash my hands before and after handling the raw foods and keep the preparation of the seafoods away from other foods. The utensils are thoroughly washed before reusing. In the kitchen I always remember the old proverb, 'A rotten fish pollutes the whole kitchen'.

Fish Basics

Rainbow Trout

Haddock

Mackerel

Salmon

Cod

Halibut

My rule of thumb for fresh fish is to cook or freeze it as soon as possible. When buying fish, I look for bright, clear eyes – they should never be dull – and red or rosy gills. The skin should be shiny and the flesh moist, firm, glistening and plump. Fish and shellfish should have the fresh smell of the sea – they should never smell overly fishy or of ammonia. It's always funny to think that fish is the only food that when spoiled smells of itself!

If you have to store it, rinse in cold water, pat dry and place, covered, at the bottom of a fridge chilled at below 4°C. I always avoid placing raw fish or shellfish in a fridge or chiller where it can drip on other foods. Don't be frightened of fish labelled 'fresh frozen' at sea. This can taste better than fresh or wet fish that has been kept on ice for many days at sea. Some of today's fishing boats use a blast-freezer to freeze fish rapidly and to a very low temperature. This preserves the texture of the fish and locks in the flavour by maintaining the firmness of the flesh.

There's not as great variety of fish available today, as we all must be careful to only use sustainable species, but don't worry, there are some delicious fish readily available.

Salmon

You are on safe ground with Atlantic salmon farmed round Scotland, and you should be able to get these in fresh fillets or whole fish. Farmed salmon sometimes get a bad press. This is down to individual cases of mismanagement, which can be found in any farming industry. Also, we must remember that fish farming on the west coast of Scotland is new in comparison to land farming, which has been refined over centuries. Our salmon farmers work really hard to bring this wonderful food to your table. In a recent survey, Scottish salmon was voted amongst the best available.

Rainbow trout
People sometimes look down their nose at rainbow trout, but it is one of the world's perfect foods. Like the salmon it is rich in Omega-3 fatty acids.

Haddock
A haddock in prime condition is an amazing fish, both as a fish dish on its own or smoked and used as an ingredient in a multitude of recipes. The best haddock tends to be frozen at sea, as the haddock grounds are far from land.

Cod
Not highly regarded by many 'afishionados', but it still holds true that you can't beat 'a nice piece of cod'. There is a reason why at one time the prosperity of the fishing industry was based on the cod.

Mackerel
All round our coast mackerel are numerous in the summer

and easily caught. Like the salmon and rainbow trout they
are an oil-rich fish full of Omega-3 oils. Delicious if cooked
and eaten fresh from the sea, but be careful, the oily flesh
spoils quickly.

Halibut
The halibut farm on the Isle of Gigha is the only one of
its kind in Scotland. The farm produces a fully sustainable
organic product. Even the sea water is pumped by power
from the island's own windfarm. Halibut is a wonderful
tasting premium fish with firm, flaky white flesh.

Preparing fish
There are a few basic rules that I rely on when preparing
fish. If a fish is being cooked whole it must always be gutted
and cleaned thoroughly. Gutting means the internal organs
of the fish are removed and the body cavity of the fish
washed. I'll take off any remaining slime by scraping the
skin of the fish with the blade of a knife and washing the
fish again.

If you're using a whole fillet, which is the complete
side of a fish cut away, make sure all the bones have been
removed. My mum, who's in charge of production at our
smokehouse, taught me a trick for removing those final
bones. Run a fingers down the inside of the fillet. Any
remaining bones can be felt and then pulled out with
tweezers.

Quick and Easy Ways to Cook Fish

COOKING SALMON / TROUT / HADDOCK: BASIC METHODS

Apart from being a wonderful ingredient in many recipes salmon is a perfect food to rustle up for a quick and tasty treat. Here are four popular methods for cooking it. They are each simple, delicious and add their own variations of taste and texture.

When using these methods, use 2 portions of fish, each about 200g (7oz). This serves 2 people.

Grilling

This is a very popular way to cook fish as it seals in the moisture and flavour.

Heat the grill. Oil both sides of the salmon fillets and season. Place under the grill in a baking tray, skin-side up. Grill for 4 to 5 minutes until the skin is crisp.

Turn the portions over and gently grill for 3 more minutes until cooked.

Poaching

For a moist and tender result, poaching is perfect.

Using a deep pan, add 250ml (½pt) of white wine, a teaspoon of peppercorns, 2 bay leaves, a stick of celery, a teaspoon of chopped parsley and a pinch of sea salt.

Add about 750ml (1¼pt) of boiling water, add the fish and gently simmer for about 10 minutes with the lid on.

Put the salmon portions in the pan and poach with the lid on for 10 minutes.

Pan-frying

The anglers' favourite. Fishermen love to think of returning home and popping the catch in the frying pan.

Season and lightly oil a non-stick frying pan over a medium heat. Add the portions skin-side down and cook for 4 minutes until the skin is really crisp. Turn them over and cook for about 2 minutes until the flesh is cooked.

Roasting

Fish doesn't benefit from high oven temperatures. Heat the oven to 180°C/350°F/gas 4. Oil the base of a baking tray adding a pinch of salt and pepper. Place the fish portions skin-side up in the tray so the flesh sits in the seasoned oil. Roast for 15 minutes. For a finishing touch gently lift the two pieces of skin from the portions, give them a twist and return the skin to the oven for another 10 minutes. Then serve the fish with the crispy skins on top (this only works if the skins have been de-scaled!).

COOKING FRESH MACKEREL

Make three cuts at the thickest part to allow the heat to penetrate. Rub the fish all over with cooking oil. Rub the body cavity with salt and put in a tbsp of chopped parsley and chives. Grill until all the flesh has turned from translucent to milky white and it comes away easily from the bone.

Quick and Easy Ways
with Smoked Fish

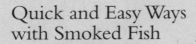

SMOKE HOUSE

As well as fresh or frozen fish a variety of smoking techniques have been perfected over the years to produce delicious-tasting foods that make meals in themselves or can be used as the most amazing ingredients.

Cold smoking is a traditional Scottish method of preserving fish and works wonderfully well with trout or salmon. Although not cooked in the traditional sense, cold-smoked trout and salmon is a ready-to-eat finished product that needs no further cooking. Cold smoking is a Scottish craft with many subtle variations, much the same as whisky-making. All smokeries have their own secrets, and that's what makes them special.

The other method of smoking is the hot smoke or 'smoke roast'. Smoking at a higher temperature both smokes and cooks the fish at the same time. This gives the final food the usual flaky texture of cooked fish. You can eat hot-smoked salmon both hot and cold. If you are using it in a recipe it's normally added towards the end so as not to double cook.

Cold-smoked salmon

Slice a fresh bagel in half and toast. Spread on cream cheese and then lay slices of Tobermory Smoked Salmon on each half. Slice a red onion into thin, circular slices. Lay a few thin slices of red onion on top of the salmon with some capers and then sprinkle with lemon juice.

Cold-smoked trout

For a great taste experience, eat Tobermory trout in wafer-thin slices on brown bread and butter with a sprinkling of lemon juice and black pepper.

Hot-smoked/smoke-roasted salmon

Eat hot-smoked salmon either cold with salad or warm. If eating warm, always add the smoked salmon to the dish near the end so as not to re-cook.

Smoked haddock

Smoked haddock is a raw product that needs to be cooked. Undyed (white) fillets of smoked haddock are a perfect breakfast dish. Poach in milk in the microwave for 4 minutes, or if poaching on the hob, poach for 5 to 7 minutes. You want the flesh to be able to flake away when pressed with a fork. Serve with a runny poached egg for a truly Scottish breakfast experience.

Quick and Easy Ways to Prepare and Cook Shellfish

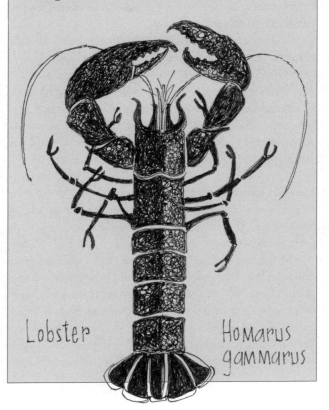

Lobster

Homarus gammarus

To make life simple I say shellfish when talking about all seafood other than fish. This includes crustaceans, such as lobsters, crabs and prawns, and molluscs, such as scallops, oysters and mussels. Before I chat about shellfish it's very important to understand that once a shellfish dies the flesh deteriorates quickly. This is why shellfish is mostly shipped either live or frozen.

To check the freshness of crustaceans use the 'tail flick' test. Pull the tail straight, and if it flicks back strongly it's a pass! Good crabs and lobsters should feel 'heavy' for their size. Molluscs must have tightly closed, undamaged shells. Cook shellfish as fresh as possible and cooking takes very little time. If overcooked it loses its succulent quality. We are very lucky today as shellfish are numerous and not endangered. Here are some of my very favourites.

Mussels (rope grown)
Rope-grown mussels are perhaps the most environmentally perfect food. Put ropes in the sea and the mussels grow on them ready for harvesting.

Mussels in the shell are cooked live. A one-kilogram (2lb 4oz) bag of mussels will do two people for a starter course. Separate out any open mussels. If they stay open when tapped, discard them as they are dead. Scrape off any barnacles and wash in cold water. Pull away the fibrous 'beard' (used to anchor the mussel) just prior to cooking and not earlier, as removing it can kill the mussel. To a pot, add half an onion, a knob of butter, about a teaspoon of chopped parsley and a crushed garlic clove. Add 250ml (½pt) of white wine, then a kilo of cleaned mussels. Bring to the boil. Cover the pot with a lid and steam for 5–7 minutes until the mussels are open and plump. Throw away any that have not opened, as they were already dead before cooking.

King scallops (often known locally as clams)
These are wonderful eating. The king scallop comes in the familiar scallop-shaped shell, one side of which is curved and the other flat. To open a fresh scallop, hold the scallop in your hand with the flat side up and the curved edge in your palm with the hinge at the tips of your fingers. Insert the end of a round-tipped knife into the opening to the side of the hinge, where there should be a gap in the shell. Work the knife towards you against the inside of the flat shell to open the two halves and cut the adductor muscle which attaches the scallop to the shell. Lift it off the top shell. Cut through the adductor and pull away the black intestinal sac and all the yellow frilly membrane. Cut the white scallop and orange coral, also known as roe, from the shell and wash (to make your life easier, scallops can of course be bought already opened (shucked) and cleaned).

Pan-fry king scallops in a little oil and butter in a hot pan for between one and three minutes, turning once. (Rapeseed oil is my favourite, but olive, vegetable or sunflower oil are all good alternatives.) It is good to put the oil in first as the pan is very hot. I add the butter in the last 30 seconds. Simply serve with a wedge of lemon and tartare sauce. Overcooked scallops become rubbery.

Queen scallops (known locally as queenies)

Smaller that the king scallop, and with a slightly different flavour, queenies are mostly sold just as meat, with no coral.

Finely slice up 2 rashers of streaky smoked bacon and drop into a hot oil-free non-stick pan. Cook until the bacon bits are crisp and golden. Remove the bacon bits, keeping the heat on. Add the scallops to the remaining bacon fat and sear each scallop for about a minute on each side. Pour in the juice of half a lemon and loosen any bits that are sticking to the bottom of the pan. Put the scallops on a plate, cover with the juices and add the bacon bits. Serve hot.

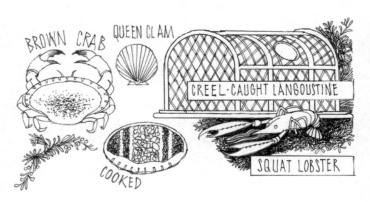

BROWN CRAB

QUEEN CLAM

CREEL-CAUGHT LANGOUSTINE

COOKED

SQUAT LOBSTER

Oysters

Oysters are sold live and it takes about four years to produce them from seed. When you are buying oysters, choose ones with the shells tightly shut. Keep them chilled, curved side down, in a dish covered with a damp cloth. Don't keep the oysters in water. To open (shuck) an oyster, hold the curved side of the shell down in a thick cloth with the hinge facing towards you. Insert the point of a knife where the shells join at the hinge by pushing and twisting downwards. Slice under the inside surface of the top shell with the knife. Cutting through the heel of the shell loosens the top shell. Run the knife along the rim of the shell to remove the top shell. Loosen the oyster flesh. Top Tip: the local oyster farmer, Gordy Turnbull, taught me to flip the meat after opening the oyster. This makes it look plumper and more delicious.

Shucked oysters are ready to eat. Eating an oyster is very much about the ritual. Display the open oysters on a heaped bed of crushed ice with slices of lemon or Tabasco and strands of seaweed.

Langoustines

Langoustines are small, slim, orange lobsters often known as Dublin Bay prawns. Try always to use creel-caught langoustines. This helps support a traditional, sustainable fishery. There's no getting away from it, langoustines are absolutely delicious. Unlike larger lobsters, which change colour from blue to orange when cooked, they are orange and remain so when cooked.

Put the langoustines in a covered pot of boiling salty water for no more than three minutes. From a whole cooked langoustine take off the head. Squeeze along the length of the body and then break open the shell from the underside with your fingers. Squeeze again and pull out the tail from the remaining shell. Langoustine can be eaten with or without the vein that runs down the inside of the flesh. To remove it you will need a small sharp knife. Holding the meat, back side up, run the knife down the length of the prawn. This will expose the vein. Use your finger or the tip of the knife to pull the vein out and then wash. The meat is ready to eat or use in your favourite recipe.

Lobster

Hebridean creel-caught lobsters are the ultimate luxury seafood, and as such are a highly-priced item. Many people find it hard to believe the blue colour of a live lobster. The lobster only turns red when cooked. They can be purchased live or ready cooked. If you buy a live lobster, make sure the claws have rubber bands on them, or you could get a nasty nip. Keep the live lobster in the fridge wrapped in a damp cloth and cook on the day of purchase. Put the lobster in the freezer for 15–30 minutes prior to cooking to sedate the lobster without freezing the meat.

In a pot of boiling water a 750g (1lb 10oz) lobster takes

about 15 to 20 minutes to cook (add two minutes for each additional 100g (4oz) in weight). After cooking, cool quickly to avoid over-cooking. Pull off the claws in order to crack them open and remove the luscious white meat. Pull off the tail. One small fact to remember if you are cutting a lobster tail for the first time: it's easier to split the tail by cutting through the hard top shell first rather than the soft underside.

Common edible crab (brown crab)

This is the familiar big pinkish-brown crab. They can be purchased live, ready-cooked or as crab meat extracted from the shell. I find collecting the crab meat from the crab quite therapeutic but a lot of hard work. Given the chance, I always purchase the picked crab meat. This comes in white, brown or mixed.

If you do feel like having a go at a whole crab, cook the crab in large pan of boiling water salted with about 30g (1oz) of salt per litre (1¾pt) of water. A 1kg (2lb 4oz) crab will cook in about 18 minutes (add a minute for every further 100g (4oz)).

RAZOR CLAMS

OR SPOOTS

MUSSELS

Squat lobsters (squatties)

These are a hidden treasure in our fisherman's by-catch. Sweet, delicious and amazingly good value. They are very quick and easy – boil in salted water for 50 seconds and no longer, plunge straight into iced water to stop further cooking. Enjoy with our seafood sauce (recipe page 92).

Razor clams (known locally as spoots)

The razor clam, so named because it resembles an old-fashioned cut-throat razor, can be gathered by hand at low spring tides. Hunting them is called spooting. The trick is to walk slowly backwards over the sand. When the 'spoot' detects the footsteps they burrow down in the sand, leaving behind a small spout of water and a hole. This alerts the spooter and a quick dig should catch the clam. Razor clams are very good eating.

Add the razor clams, a tablespoon of olive oil and half a glass of dry white wine to a steaming pan of water. Cook, covered, for two minutes.

These last few pages have been a very rough guide to the shellfish you may come across both in shops and on the shore. If you are at all doubtful about eating it, please always check locally. It's important to do this as some shellfish become unsuitable for eating at certain times of the year, or due to natural events such as some types of plankton bloom.

Our Favourite Fish Recipes

Hot-Smoked Salmon Pâté

A summer starter or serve as a canapé on some mini oatcakes.

Serves 4
200g (7oz) hot-smoked salmon
1 tbsp horseradish sauce
Small handful of chopped chives and chopped dill
Juice of 1 lemon
400–500g (14oz–1lb 2oz) cream cheese

Firstly flake the hot-smoked salmon into a food processor and blend the fish. Now add the horseradish, chives, dill and lemon juice and pulse until mixed. Finally add the cream cheese a little at a time, until all mixed in and smooth.

Serve with toasted sourdough, wedges of lemon and black pepper.

Classic Smoked Trout Pâté

Add this to a grazing platter with some nice crackers.
One of my go-to favourites when having the girls round.
Also makes a great canapé.

Serves 4

200g (7oz) cold-smoked trout trimmings
1 tbsp horseradish sauce
Small handful of chopped chives and chopped dill
Juice of 1 lemon
400g–500g (14oz–1lb 2oz) cream cheese
100g (4 oz) hot-smoked trout to flake at the end (optional)

Put the smoked trout into a food processor and blend.
Add the horseradish, chives, dill and lemon juice and
pulse until mixed. Then add the cream cheese a little at a
time until it is all mixed in and smooth.

To make the pâté 'rustic' I like to flake in a little hot-
smoked trout at the end.

Serve with toasted sourdough, wedges of lemon and
black pepper.

Mull-en Skink

Our local twist on the classic Cullen Skink. Scallops and smoked haddock soup for all seafood lovers.

Serves 4–6

1 white onion, diced
½ leek, chopped
1 tbsp olive oil
1 glass of white wine
3 medium to large potatoes, peeled and cubed
1 litre (1¾pt) chicken stock
500ml (17 fl oz) double cream
6 fresh scallops, hand-caught if possible
200g (7oz) undyed smoked haddock, cut in to small
    1cm (½in) cubes
Salt and pepper

Sweat the onion and leek in the oil in a large pan until soft. Add the white wine and let it reduce until the liquid is gone. Put in the cubed potatoes and the chicken stock and simmer for 15 minutes until the potatoes are cooked. Add the double cream and let it heat through.

Cut the scallops in half and put into the broth along with the smoked haddock, poaching for a few minutes until they are cooked.

Season to taste and serve with crusty white bread or an Isle of Mull Cheddar Crouton (see p. 95).

'The Morning After' Smoked Salmon and Scrambled Eggs

A recipe from my mum's cousin Laurie Mill, a yacht chef with great taste. He says: 'My favourite recipe using cold-smoked salmon. It's simple but luxuriates on the discerning palate like fresh peaches and cream.'

Serves 4
4 slices brown bread
12 eggs
30ml (1fl oz) double cream
Freshly ground black pepper
100g unsalted butter
100g (4oz) cold-smoked salmon cut into 4 pieces
½ tsp sea salt
A small bunch of fresh parsley

Toast and butter the bread. Break the eggs in a bowl and whisk with the cream and 3 turns of the pepper grinder.

Melt butter in a pan and add the egg mixture. Heat gently, drawing the mixture slowly from the sides of the pan into the middle with a wooden spoon (do not whisk).

When half-cooked, fold in the salmon and continue drawing the mixture from the sides until it is almost set and slightly wet. Add salt to taste.

Serve on buttered toast and garnish with a sprig of parsley.

Scottish Savoury Pancakes with Smoked Trout and Horseradish Cream

These little bites of heaven are now a Christmas tradition. Serve as a canapé when the family arrive, with some chilled bubbly.

This recipe makes 24 mini pancakes for canapés or 8–10 larger pancakes to serve as a starter for 4 people.

100g (4oz) caster sugar
250g (9oz) self-raising flour
2 eggs
A splash of milk
Fresh dill and chives, chopped (save some chives for the garnish)
Horseradish sauce
200g (8oz) cold-smoked trout
Pinch of salt
1 lemon cut into wedges to serve

First make your pancakes. Put the sugar and flour in a bowl with a pinch of salt, add the eggs and whisk. The mixture will be very thick at first, add the milk bit by bit to thin it slightly. You want the consistency to be like a thick batter or almost like double cream, so you will not need much milk. Chop the herbs up finely and add to the batter, then stir so they are evenly mixed through.

Use a heavy non-stick frying pan and test the pan is hot enough by adding a small amount of batter – you should see air bubbles come up through the batter when it's at the right heat. Spoon a small bit of the mixture into the pan one at a time to make perfect pancakes! The pancakes are ready to be flipped over when air comes through the top and little bubbles are visible.

When the pancakes are ready put on a serving platter. Top with a small spread of horseradish sauce for the trout to stick, then add a nice ribbon of smoked trout.

Finish with a blob of the horseradish sauce on top with some chives and black pepper. Serve with a lemon wedge to squeeze.

Smoked Trout Roulade

My cousin Helen's legendary roulade. A Hebridean Lodge special loved by the locals of Tobermory.

Serves 4

500g (1lb 2oz) cold-smoked trout
500g (1lb 2oz) cream cheese
Juice and zest of 1 lemon
½ red onion, finely diced
2 tbsp gherkins, chopped

1 tbsp fresh dill, chopped
1 tbsp fresh chives, chopped
3 sheets gelatine soaking in water
Lumpfish caviar to garnish

In a blender mix 200g (7oz) of the trout, cream cheese, and lemon juice and zest. Add the red onion, gherkin and herbs. Drain the gelatine and heat in a microwave or stir in a saucepan over a very low heat until melted. Add the gelatine to the mixture and blend. Put into a fridge to start setting.

Lay out cling film about 40cms (15in) long. Place the remaining slices of trout in a 30 × 20cm (12 × 8in) rectangle. Put the trout and cream cheese mixture into a piping bag and pipe along the nearest long edge. Using cling film to help, roll the trout around the mixture into a tight sausage shape. Twist and knot each end of the cling film and put in the fridge to finish setting.

Cut off the ends of the cling film and remove. Slice the roulade into small discs. Serve on miniature oatcakes with lumpfish caviar and a sprig of dill.

Scallops with Mango Salad

Add some Caribbean zing to your local scallops. I sometimes like to make this as a main course by increasing the number of scallops and serving with rice.

Serves 2
Olive oil
Zest and juice of 1 lime
2cm (1in) cube of ginger, grated
2–3 tbsp coriander, chopped
6 scallops
2 ripe mangoes
Watercress
Spring onions

Put three tablespoons of oil, the lime zest, lime juice and ginger in a bowl and whisk together.

Season to taste and add two or three tablespoons of fresh coriander.

Put the scallops in a bowl and coat with olive oil. Season and then sear the scallops in a hot frying pan for half a minute each side.

Arrange the scallops, slices of fresh mango and watercress on a plate. Drizzle over the dressing and scatter with fine slices of spring onion.

Smoked Scallops and Roast Beetroot Salad

An earthy salad with the added luxury of the smoked scallops.

Serves 2
2 beetroot
2 small sprigs rosemary
Mixed lettuce leaves including rocket
Extra virgin olive oil
Balsamic vinegar
4 smoked scallops
4 shavings of parmesan
Coriander, chopped
Freshly ground black pepper

For the dressing
1 tsp onion, grated
½ tsp horseradish, grated
¼ tsp Dijon mustard
A splash of lemon juice
Salt and pepper to taste
300ml (½pt) double cream

Trim the green stalks to within half a centimetre of the top of the beetroot. Wash, dry and make a small incision with a knife at the top of each beetroot. Put a sprig of rosemary in each cut, and wrap each beetroot in foil.

Cook in a moderate oven (180°C/350°F/gas 4) until tender and the skins come off in your fingers, about 30 to 45 minutes. Allow to cool, top, tail and peel. Cut into six wedges each.

For the dressing, put all the ingredients together and whisk until the consistency of custard. Chill.

To assemble, dress four plates lightly with the lettuce leaves. Drizzle with the olive oil and balsamic vinegar. Scatter over the beetroot wedges. Cut scallops in half horizontally and place these on top. Cover with the dressing, top with the parmesan shavings and chopped coriander. Finish with a good crack of black pepper.

Tobermory Smoked Trout and Horseradish

Good flavours to serve with cold-smoked trout or salmon are those with a kick, such as citrus or horseradish.

Serves 4
2 spring onions, finely chopped
½ cucumber, diced
25g (1oz) coriander, chopped
200g (7oz) cold-smoked trout
250g (8oz) natural yoghurt
1 tbsp horseradish sauce
Lime slices to garnish

Mix the spring onion, cucumber and coriander in a dish. Divide the smoked trout slices on four plates and heap the cucumber mix over the smoked trout slices.

Mix up the yoghurt and horseradish and pour over the salad and trout. Serve with brown bread and lime slices.

Smoked Salmon BLT

Smoked salmon and bacon . . . who knew this would be a mouth–watering combo.

---

2 thick slices of crusty bread or a fresh roll
1 tbsp mayonnaise with a squeeze of lemon
50g (2oz) cold-smoked salmon
1 portion of lettuce or watercress
2 rashers smoked bacon, cooked and crispy
2 slices of big tomatoes (not wee cherry tomatoes!)

Assemble all together in the bread or roll. I do in the order above, but you might want to switch them around for a different experience.

Hot-smoked Salmon, Avocado, Chilli and Crème Fraîche Toasted Sandwich

My cousin Helen helps me again by providing this recipe. I really love this fresh combo of the avocado, coriander and hot-smoked salmon.

Makes 1 sandwich
2 tbsp crème fraîche
¼ a red onion, finely chopped
1 tsp fresh coriander, chopped
Zest and juice of ½ lime
½ red chilli, de-seeded and finely chopped
½ ripe avocado, chopped
100g (4oz) hot-smoked salmon
3 slices of good quality bread of your choice

Mix the crème fraîche, red onion, coriander, the zest and juice of the lime, the chilli and avocado. Flake in the Cajun salmon. Toast the bread, butter it and spread the mix onto two slices. Make up into a three-tiered sandwich. We serve with homemade chipped potatoes and salad.

Smoked Salmon Straws

Thank you, Mum, for introducing me to this amazing snack. You can eat them with dips or even dunk them into a nice creamy cauliflower soup. Smoked salmon rashers are best as they are packed with flavour.

Makes 10–12 straws
250g (9oz) ready-rolled puff pastry
25g (1oz) gruyère, grated
25g (1oz) parmesan, grated
50g (2oz) smoked salmon or trout rashers, finely chopped
A pinch of cayenne
1 egg yolk mixed with 1 tbsp of milk

Preheat the oven to 190°C/375°F/gas 5.

Roll out the pastry as thinly as possible in a rectangle about 30 × 50cm (12 × 20in). Position the long side facing you and scatter the cheeses, salmon rashers and cayenne over the upper half of the pastry leaving a wee border at the top. Brush the border with the egg-yolk mixture and fold up the lower half of the pastry over the upper half. Press the edges together then lightly roll the pastry again to seal.

Cut vertically into 2cm (1in) strips. Holding both ends of a strip, twist four or five times and lay on non-stick baking tray, pinching the ends together so they don't unravel. Bake for 12–15 minutes until golden.

Smoked Salmon Terrine

Keep in mind when slicing this to have a really sharp knife. We serve ours with rough oatcakes or Melba toast.

Serves 4–6

400g (14oz) cold-smoked salmon, long slices	2 tsp fresh dill (or 1 tsp dried)
200g (7oz) cream cheese	25g (1oz) gherkins, finely chopped
150g (5oz) hot-smoked salmon	Freshly ground black pepper
Zest of 2 lemons	300ml (½pt) double cream

Line a 900g (2lb) loaf tin with cling film, allowing some excess cling film to hang over the edges. Line the inside with the long salmon slices leaving no gaps and a slight overhang to fold at the end.

Whizz the cheese and the rest of the salmon until well combined. Empty into a large bowl and add the lemon zest, dill, gherkins and plenty of black pepper.

In a separate bowl, whip the double cream until it is firm then fold into the fish mixture.

Spoon into the lined tin and press down firmly. Bring the overhanging salmon strips up to cover the top of the mixture. Fold over the cling film and then wrap the whole tin tightly in more cling film and chill for at least 4 hours or preferably overnight.

When ready to serve, remove the cling film and invert over a serving plate.

Smoked Mussels with Garlic

The new super-duper 'bar snack'. Impress your guests
with some smoked mussel canapés on arrival.

200g (7oz) smoked mussels (you can use tinned)
Juice of ¼ lemon
200g (7oz) mayonnaise
1 large garlic clove
20–25 mussel shells, cleaned
Fresh dill to garnish (optional)
20–25 cocktail sticks

Each time I steam mussels I keep some shells back to use
for recipes like these – it's a really fun way to dish up
these delights.

Separate the cleaned mussel shells and arrange them
on a nice platter.

Add the lemon juice to the mayonnaise with the
crushed garlic clove and mix.

Put a small spoon of the mayo mix in each of the
mussel shells, and place one large or a couple of the
smaller smoked mussels on the mayonnaise. Top with a
small sprig of dill on each canapé and serve with a
cocktail stick.

The Ultimate Crab Brioche

The brioche trend started for me when I visited the Borough Market in London. Lobster rolls seemed to be a new food on the block. After my first bite I was sold. The tangy sauce coating the shellfish mixed with the sweet buttery bread was a new sensation. Here is my version, Crab Brioche.

Makes 4 rolls

150g (5oz) white crab meat	1 tbsp salad cream
150g (5oz) brown crab meat	Bunch of spring onions, chopped
Juice of ½ lemon	4 brioche rolls
1 tbsp mayonnaise	Butter
1 tsp tomato ketchup	Iceberg lettuce

Mix the white and brown crab meat in a bowl and add the lemon juice. In a small separate bowl, mix the mayonnaise, tomato sauce and salad cream, until you get a lovely pink seafood sauce. Add the seafood sauce to the crab mixture along with the chopped spring onions. Mix well.

Slice and butter your brioche rolls. Spread the crab mixture evenly over the rolls and top with washed crispy lettuce.

Another option is to slice these up for party food or, if you get smaller rolls, make 8 small sliders.

Val's Devilled Crab

Spread all over crusty bread. The thicker you spread it, the better! Val is my mum's friend and a master in the kitchen. We visit her house every Christmas Eve and I look forward to her devilled crab every year.

Serves 2–4
1 small onion, finely chopped
Knob of butter
300g mixed crab meat
4 heaped tbsp fresh breadcrumbs
1tsp Worcestershire sauce
A few shakes of tabasco
1 tsp grain mustard
150ml (¼pt) double cream
Salt and pepper
Parmesan, grated

Soften the onion in the butter and remove from the heat. Next add the crab, half the breadcrumbs, the Worcestershire sauce, Tabasco, mustard and cream, and season with salt and pepper.

Put into a shallow baking dish and top with the rest of the breadcrumbs and a little parmesan. Bake in the oven at 200°C/400°F/gas 6 for 15 minutes.

Smokie Trout Rasher Soda Bread

Quickest (and tastiest) bread EVER. Having last-minute guests over for lunch? This recipe is for you. We supply what we call Smokie Trout Rashers, the top cut of cold-smoked strips of trout, at the Smokehouse. If you can't get these, use any cold-smoked trout.

500g (1lb 2oz) wholemeal flour
2 tsp salt
1 tsp baking soda
1 tbsp chives, chopped
60g (2oz) gruyère cheese

125g (4oz) Smokie Trout Rashers or cold-smoked trout strips, snipped into small pieces
375ml (12fl oz) buttermilk
2 tsp butter, melted
1 tbsp porridge oats

Preheat the oven to 200°C/400°F/gas 6.

Put all the dry ingredients in a bowl, add the fish, chives and cheese and mix. Make a well in the centre and pour in the buttermilk and butter. Bring the dough together with a fork.

Scatter the porridge oats on a smooth surface. Empty the dough from the bowl and knead together until it holds its shape. Transfer the dough to a greased baking sheet and cut a cross shape on the top.

Place in the hot oven and cook for 10 minutes. Then rotate the baking sheet, turn the oven down to 190°C/375°F/gas 5 and cook for another 30 minutes.

Cool on a wire tray.

Smoked Salmon Brunch Hash

Sunday brunch is a great time to use hot-smoked salmon. This recipe is very popular with us as it is really different and quick, and comes in handy especially if, like me, you do it to use up those extra potatoes from the night before. Serve family style in a big bowl so everyone can help themselves.

Serves 4
400g (14oz) new potatoes, boiled
Olive oil
100g (4oz) baby spinach
4 spring onions, roughly chopped
8 asparagus spears, chopped to 1cm lengths
10g (½oz) butter
Pinch of salt and pepper
4 large free-range eggs
300g (10oz) hot-smoked salmon (or trout works just as well)

To serve:
1 tbsp roughly torn dill
Sour cream
Wedges of lemon
Horseradish sauce

Cut your pre-boiled new potatoes in half, and in a large frying pan fry them inside down in some oil to give them a nice golden crust. Add in the spinach, chopped spring onion and asparagus to fry lightly.

Add the butter to the pan and season with salt and pepper. Make four spaces in the pan and break in the eggs to fill the spaces. Turn the heat down and cook until the eggs turn white at the bottom. Then turn off the heat and put the pan under the grill to cook the top of the eggs.

When the eggs are cooked (I like to have runny yolks) flake the hot-smoked salmon on top along with some dill, sour cream, a little horseradish sauce and a nice wedge of lemon on the side.

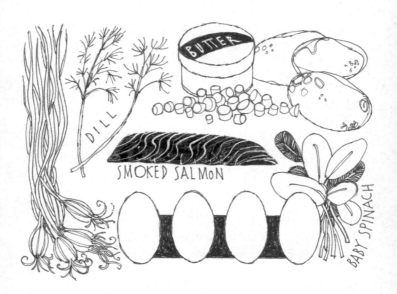

Malaysian Mussels

The flavour of the East meets the West (coast). For extra spice, add more chillies.

Serves 4

Olive oil
5 spring onions, finely chopped
1cm (½in) cube fresh ginger
2 cloves of garlic, crushed
1 red chilli
Fresh coriander

1 tbsp Thai red curry paste
Tin of coconut milk
1 lime
2kg (4½lb) fresh cleaned mussels, in the shell

Put a splash of oil in a deep enough pot to hold the 2 kilos of mussels and add the spring onions, ginger, garlic, chilli and finely chopped coriander stalks, putting the leaves aside for garnish later. Fry for a couple of minutes. Add the curry paste and coconut milk.

Cut the lime in half and squeeze the lime over the pot to get most of the juice out, then put the two halves in and bring to a simmer. Rinse the mussels and add to the pot.

Put a lid on and allow the mussels to steam until the shells are fully open (remember to remove any mussels that haven't opened). I like to give the pot a shake or a stir four minutes in.

Scatter with fresh coriander and serve with rice or crusty bread.

Seafood Lasagne

This recipe was given to me by head chef Ramy from MacGochans, in Tobermory. We love making it at home topped with cheddar.

Serves 6

½ pack salted butter
Plain flour (about 3 tbsp)
300ml (½pt) fish stock
600ml (1pt) water
2 tsp garlic purée
Pinch of fresh tarragon
Pinch of fresh dill
1 onion, finely chopped
300ml (½pt) single cream
300g (10oz) mature cheddar cheese, grated
Salt and pepper
10 lasagne sheets
4 smoked haddock fillets
200g (7oz) cold-smoked salmon
350g (12oz) Atlantic prawns, cooked and peeled

To make the seafood sauce, melt all the butter in a pan and make the roux by adding enough plain flour until the mixture is smooth and thick. Add the fish stock and hand-whisk until smooth. Continue whisking and add the water.

Stir through the garlic, tarragon and dill and sprinkle the raw finely-chopped onion into the sauce. The cream should be added a bit at a time until the consistency is thin but not watery. Add half the grated cheese now as the final step to the seafood sauce and season with salt and pepper.

To make the lasagne, first grease a baking tray of suitable depth. Layer the base with sauce, then put on a layer of the pasta sheets to cover the sauce and add more sauce on top. Place the raw smoked haddock fillets side by side in the tray and cover with a thick layer of the sauce. Add a second layer of pasta sheets followed by a thin layer of sauce. Cover with the smoked salmon and all the prawns. Finish with a final layer of pasta and cover with the remaining sauce and the rest of the grated cheese. Cook uncovered at 190°C/375°F/gas 5 for 30–35 minutes.

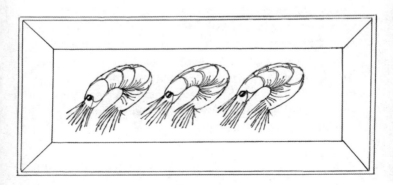

Fresh Mackerel Ceviche

My dad has a fishing tackle shop on Tobermory Main
Street. Often keen anglers come in with their catch to
show him. One particular family had great luck and
brought in a haul of fresh mackerel. He asked what they
were going to do with them and they wrote down this
recipe for him to try.

___

Serves 2 as a main or 4 as a starter
4 fresh mackerel, filleted and skinned, finely chopped and seasoned
    with salt to taste
Juice of 4 limes
2 garlic cloves, crushed and chopped
½ red onion, very finely chopped
Bunch of fresh coriander
1 fresh red chilli, thinly sliced

___

Put the mackerel into a bowl and cover with the lime
juice, garlic and onion. Make sure all the flesh is covered
with the lime juice, as this 'cooks' the fish. Leave in the
fridge to marinate for 1 hour 30 minutes. The flesh will
turn from pinky grey to white when it is done.

Serve with chopped coriander and fresh chilli. Some
people like this served like a dip with some tortilla chips,
or with a salad as a starter.

Smoked Mussels Wrapped in Sole

An easy meal with a touch of culinary genius.

Serves 2
2 skinned fillets of sole
16 smoked mussels
1 tbsp tarragon, chopped
150ml (¼pt) fish stock
150ml (¼pt) dry white wine
4 tbsp of crème fraîche
Salt and pepper

Place fish skin side down and lightly season. Then put half the mussels on each sole fillet, away from the edges. Sprinkle the tarragon over the fish and mussels and then roll to wrap the mussels in the sole. Place in an oven dish with the fish stock and wine and close the lid. Bake in the oven at 180°C/350°F/gas 4 for 25 minutes.

When cooked remove the rolled fillets and keep warm.

Simmer on the hob until the cooking liquor is reduced by half and stir in the crème fraîche. Cut each rolled fillet into two pieces and arrange on the sauce.

Serve with steamed greens and new potatoes.

Hot-Smoked Salmon Pasta Salad

A quick and easy lunch for all the family or the perfect
addition to the BBQ salad bar.

Serves 2 to 4
400g (14oz) dried penne pasta
1 red pepper, chopped
2 spring onions, chopped
200g (7oz) tinned sweetcorn, drained
200g (7oz) hot-smoked salmon, chopped or flaked
4 tbsp Hellmann's mayonnaise
4 tbsp salad cream
1 tsp horseradish sauce
A squeeze of lemon juice
1 tsp cracked black pepper

Cook the pasta according to the packet instructions.
While the pasta is cooking, add the red pepper, spring
onions, sweetcorn and salmon to your serving bowl. In a
separate bowl, mix the mayo, salad cream, horseradish and
lemon juice. Assemble by mixing the pasta with your
sauce and adding to serving bowl. Fold together and
serve. Season to taste.

Risotto of Smoked Haddock

One of our household weeklies. Tobermory Smoked
Haddock and Isle of Mull Cheddar is a winning combo
for me – they both work in harmony for most savoury,
creamy dishes. You can, of course, use your own local
favourites.

Serves 4
400g (14oz) smoked haddock
400ml (¾pt) whole milk
2 tbsp vegetable oil
Knob of butter
1 large leek, thinly sliced
300g (10oz) Arborio risotto rice
250ml dry white wine
1litre (1¾pt) hot chicken stock
100g (4oz) grated cheddar
2 tbsp chives, snipped
150ml (¼pt) double cream (optional)

Put the fish into a pan and cover with the milk. Simmer
for 4 to 5 minutes until cooked. Leave aside to cool, then
drain and flake.

In a deep, wide frying pan, heat the oil and butter
and cook the leeks on a low heat until soft but not
coloured. Turn up the heat and add the rice. Stir well to
coat the grains, then pour in the wine and stir till
absorbed.

Add the hot chicken stock a ladleful at a time, stirring it in to bring the starch out of the rice. Do this until the rice is just tender and creamy. You may not need to use all of the stock.

Flake the cooled haddock and grated cheddar into the rice, mix well and check the seasoning. Add the chives and serve. You could mix in a generous slug of double cream before adding the chives for a richer finish.

The dish can be garnished with a soft poached egg on top, steamed asparagus spears or shaved parmesan.

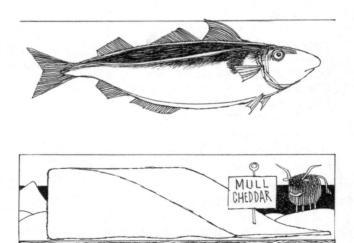

Crab and Pancetta Pasta Bake

Some upmarket comfort food right here. I like to serve mine family-style in the gratin dish for people to help themselves, with a big green dressed salad.

Serves 2
250g (9oz) penne pasta
Olive oil
100g (4oz) pancetta
30g (1oz) butter
40g (1½oz) plain flour
500ml (18fl oz) milk
1 tbsp Dijon mustard
100g (4oz) parmesan
100g (4oz) cheddar cheese
Pepper to season
200g (8oz) sourdough
4 tbsp fresh parsley
200g (8oz) crabmeat

Cook the pasta until al dente and drain. Meanwhile, fry the pancetta in olive oil until crisp. Remove to a plate with a slotted spoon, reserving the oil in the pan.

Add the butter to the pan and melt, then stir in the flour and cook for a minute. Remove from the heat and whisk in the milk, stirring until smooth. Return to the heat and bring to the boil continuing to stir until thickened. Mix in the mustard and most of the cheeses, reserving some to top the bake with. Season with pepper only.

Blitz the sourdough and parsley to breadcrumbs in a food processor.

Heat the oven to 190°C/375°F/gas 5.

Mix together the crabmeat, pancetta, cheese sauce and pasta and place in a gratin dish. Top with the breadcrumbs and remaining cheese.

Bake for 30 to 35 minutes.

Delicious!

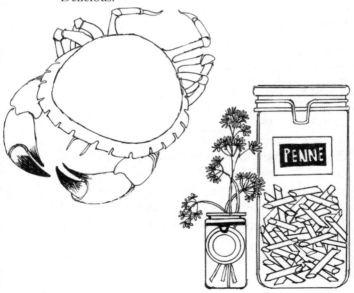

Roasted Salmon with Oriental Dressing

This recipe is my aunty Ali Rutherford's. A twist on the simple roast salmon that we love. Serve with sticky rice or noodles.

Serves 4

500g (1lb 2oz) broccoli florets
2 cloves garlic, grated or finely chopped
6 tbsp olive oil
4 salmon portions about 200g each
2 spring onions, finely chopped
1 red chilli, seeded and chopped
Thumb-sized piece of ginger, grated
2 tbsp Nam Pla (Thai fish sauce)
Zest and juice of 2 limes
2 tbsp fresh coriander, chopped
1 tbsp smooth peanut butter

Preheat the oven to 180°C/350°F/gas 4. Put the broccoli florets and grated garlic in a roasting tin with 2 tablespoons of the oil and mix together. Add the salmon portions to the broccoli mixture, cover the tin with foil and roast for 25 minutes.

Mix together the spring onions and chilli, grated ginger, Nam Pla, lime zest and juice, fresh coriander and peanut butter with 4 tbsp olive oil. Drizzle this dressing over the cooked salmon and broccoli.

Spicy Seafood, Potato and Chorizo Stew

I took this dish to all our recent street food events. It's a great winter warmer with a kick. I like to serve this with crusty bread that has been put in the oven to heat right through, and an extra thick spreading of butter is essential.

Serves 4

2 tbsp olive oil
1 onion, finely chopped
1 red chilli, chopped (leave the chilli seeds in for extra spice)
1 red pepper, chopped
Salt and pepper
175ml white wine
100g (4oz) of high quality chorizo
2 knobs of butter
400g (14oz) baby potatoes, skin on and roughly quartered
300ml (½pt) tinned chopped tomatoes
300ml (½pt) chicken stock
1 cleaned squid tube, cut into rings
500g (1lb 2oz) fresh live mussels
1 fillet of smoked haddock
4 tsp crème fraîche
8 sprigs of fresh coriander to garnish (optional)

Using a soup or stew pot, sweat the onion, chilli and red pepper in the olive oil until soft, seasoned with a pinch of salt and pepper. Add the white wine and simmer until most of it has evaporated.

Cut the chorizo into small cubes and add to the pan with the butter and baby potatoes, the tinned tomatoes and chicken stock and simmer on a low heat until the potatoes are cooked.

Clean and prep the seafood. Wash the mussels in cold water and de-beard. Discard any with broken shells or any that are open slightly. Make sure the smoked haddock does not have any bones by running your fingers down the middle of the fish. Cut out any bones and discard them and chop the smoked haddock into bite-sized chunks.

When your potatoes are fully cooked – check this by testing them with a fork to see if they are soft – add the mussels to the pot and stir. Cover the pan for 5 minutes to let the mussels cook through and begin to open. Add in the squid tubes and smoked haddock and leave to cook for a further 5–7 minutes. The seafood will be ready when the mussels are open and plump and the smoked haddock easily flakes.

Serve in bowls topped with a spoon of crème fraîche and some fresh coriander, and with warm crusty bread.

Smoked Haddock and Pancetta Carbonara

When my mum has visitors, Italian is the theme ninety per cent of the time. She always manages to put her own spin on some classic Italian dishes, and Tobermory Smoked Haddock in this dish does it perfectly.

Serves 4

400g (14oz) spaghetti
400g (14oz) smoked haddock fillets, chopped into 12 chunks
100g (4oz) pancetta
Olive oil
25g (1oz) butter
3 garlic cloves, finely chopped
3 eggs (Mum loves to use her own duck eggs for extra creaminess)
100g (4oz) parmesan
Freshly ground black pepper

Cook the spaghetti in a large pan of boiling water. Remove any bones from the haddock fillets and add the fish to the pasta for the last 5 minutes of cooking. Fry the pancetta in a tsp of olive oil till crisp, then add the butter and garlic and fry together for a minute. Whisk the eggs and the parmesan together with some black pepper.

Drain the haddock and pasta and return to the pan, tip in the egg mixture and the pancetta with a little of the pasta liquid if necessary to moisten, and heat through for one minute.

Monkfish Wrapped in Bacon with Pesto

This recipe is more a dinner party main than a family staple in my house. I have actually tried it with a number of sides, but my favourite has got to be a creamy mash and simple buttery green beans. The monkfish also works well with some nice rustic potato wedges.

Serves 4

800g–1kg (1lb 12oz–2lb) whole monkfish fillet
8 thick streaky bacon rashers
4 tbsp green or red pesto
2 tbsp olive oil
2 tbsp salted butter

Put the monkfish fillet on a large board and pat dry, then put to one side.

Spread a sheet of cling film on the board and lay all the bacon rashers out so they can be fully wrapped around the monkfish, with no gaps. If the monkfish is long and thin I cut the rashers in half. Spoon a layer of pesto over the bacon before laying the monkfish on top.

This is where your wrapping skills come in! Carefully wrap the bacon around the monkfish, trying to cover all the white flesh of the fish except the ends. Then use the cling film to wrap it all tightly together and twist the ends of the cling film to seal.

Put in the fridge for 3 hours minimum (or the night before cooking even better) to set and bind.

Preheat your oven to 200°C/400°F/gas 6, 45 minutes before serving. Then, 30 minutes before serving, put the oil into a large non-stick pan on a high heat and add the wrapped monkfish. This should sizzle straight away, and you want to turn it carefully until all the bacon has become a nice golden colour. Switch off the heat, add your butter and baste a little before transferring to a baking tray and putting it in your preheated oven for 15 minutes or more until cooked with bright white flesh showing all the way through. This timing really depends on how thick your monkfish is.

Take the monkfish out of the oven and with a very sharp knife slice it in four. Serve with your chosen sides, and enjoy.

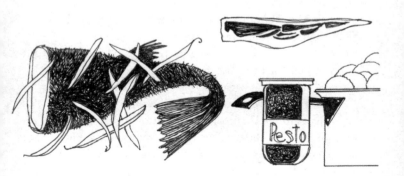

Split Langoustines in Garlic Butter

A really nice dinner party starter. I think having langoustines kicking off your dinner party menu really sets the tone for an upmarket foodie evening, and this simple recipe shows the langoustine in all its glory. It's easy for your guests to eat as you've done all the heavy lifting – no need for shells being broken open and flying all over the dining room, but it still shows off the beautiful shellfish. The feel of this dish is 'from sea to plate'.

Serves 4 as a starter (or 2 for a main course)
12 live langoustines
125g (4oz) salted butter at room temperature
4 cloves of garlic, crushed
Small bunch of parsley, finely chopped
Fresh bread for serving
1 lemon cut in 4 for serving
Ice cubes

Start by putting your live langoustines in the freezer for 15-20 minutes to 'put them to sleep'. While they are chilling, boil a pot of water, big enough for all the langoustines to be covered, and add a pinch of salt.

When the water is on a rolling boil add your langoustines and cover for 5 minutes. While they are cooking, fill your sink with cold water and add some ice cubes, if you have them, to make the water extra cold, the colder the better. After the 5 minutes are up, take the langoustines out of the pot with tongs and plunge them into the cool iced water to make sure they stop cooking.

When the langoustines are cool, place them on some kitchen paper to dry. Put them on a chopping board one at a time, and with a sharp, heavy knife split the langoustine in half from the head down to the end of the tail. Lay the half langoustines on a baking tray, shell-side down, and remove the small hard sac behind the eyes.

Make your garlic butter by putting the butter, garlic and parsley in a small bowl and mixing with a fork until all combined.

Put dollops of the garlic butter on the flesh of each of the langoustines and put under a hot grill for 3 to 4 minutes until all the butter has melted.

Plate up 6 half langoustines on each plate with a nice big chunk of bread and a slice of lemon, and drizzle the remaining garlic butter in the baking tray over each plate evenly.

Mrs Alexander's Cajun and Asparagus Pasta

This recipe was created by my friend Hannah. She wasn't a fan of fish when I first met her . . . now she is a seafood afishionado!

Serves 2

5 nests of tagliatelle pasta
6 asparagus, chopped into
    1-inch batons
Knob of butter
½ red chilli
2 cloves garlic, chopped
200ml (7fl oz) crème fraîche

2 tbsp lemon juice
Sprinkle of your favourite
    Cajun spice
Salt and pepper
80–100ml (2–3fl oz) water
200g (7oz) Cajun hot-smoked
    salmon

Put on your pasta to cook while you get on with the sauce. When the pasta is al dente, add in the asparagus to blanch for about 4 minutes and then drain. Retain 100ml of the pasta water for later. In a deep frying pan, on a medium heat, melt a knob of butter and fry the chilli and garlic for a few minutes, then add the crème fraîche, lemon juice, Cajun spice, salt and pepper. Stir on the medium heat to form the sauce and gradually add 80–100ml of the pasta water until you have a creamy consistency.

Flake the Cajun salmon and add it to the frying pan along with the cooked pasta and asparagus and mix. Serve with a sprinkle of parmesan.

Hand-caught Scallops with Bacon and Basil Butter

Serves 2 as a main course or 4 as a starter
12 hand-caught scallops, opened, cleaned and the top shell discarded
1 tbsp oil
150g (5oz) salted butter, left out at room temperature to soften
4 rashers of smoked bacon, grilled until crispy, then finely chopped
8 large basil leaves, finely chopped
Crusty bread or boiled new potatoes to serve

First, rinse your scallops under running water. Then using a spoon, scoop out the scallop meat from the shells and lay on some kitchen paper to dry.

In a frying pan add a little oil and turn up the heat. Sear the scallops for 2 minutes on each side until they are golden.

Lay the empty shells on a baking tray, inside up, and put these under the grill for 5 minutes to heat. We are going to use these as little bowls for our scallops.

Mix the butter with the cooled bacon and basil and add to the butter.

Put each of the scallops back in their shells and divide the butter between them. Put under the hot grill for a further minute until the butter has melted.

Serve with crusty bread. A warning: the shells will be incredibly hot, so use some tongs.

Tobermory Fisherman's Pie

My dad was visibly shaken when I told him I was including this recipe. He liked to think of it as his personal Tobermory treat, but what the heck, a shared secret is the best kind.

Serves 4–6
4–6 large baking potatoes, peeled and cut in to 4
1 tbsp oil
½ white onion, finely diced
½ leek, chopped into rings
300ml dry white wine
200g (7oz) cream cheese
500g (1lb 2oz) crème fraîche
2 smoked haddock fillets, bones removed and chopped into chunks
200g (7oz) smokie rashers, trout or salmon, or fresh trout or salmon, skinless and chopped into 8 chunks
8 large king prawns, raw, peeled and de-veined
2 large sprigs of dill without stalks, chopped roughly
2 tsp chives, chopped
Knob of butter
100ml (3fl oz) whole milk
Cracked black pepper (optional)
100g (4oz) cheddar, grated

Start by putting your potatoes on to boil in some salted water. Then sweat the onion and leeks in the oil in a deep pot. I like to use a Le Creuset type of cooking pot. When they have softened add a mug of white wine and leave to simmer until most of the wine has evaporated.

Now add the cream cheese and crème fraîche to the leek mixture and stir well, followed by your fish, dill and chives. Stir regularly so that it doesn't get stuck to the bottom of the pan. When it is bubbling through you can spoon it into an oven-proof dish. Set this to one side. Strain your potatoes when cooked and mash with a knob of butter and the milk until creamy and thick. Add some cracked black pepper for seasoning if you like.

Top the dish with the creamy mash. Add a spoonful at a time and fork roughly so it covers the whole pie. Sprinkle over the cheddar. Put in a preheated oven at 180°C for 20 minutes or until golden brown and bubbling.

Serve with green beans and peas.

Moules Marinière or
MULL Marinière as we like to call it!

We are really lucky on Mull as there are brilliant live mussels available from our local producer, Inverlussa, but your good local fishmonger will be fine.

Serves 4 as a starter or 2 as a main
2kg (4½lb) fresh, live, rope-grown mussels
1 large knob of butter
1 white onion, diced very small
4 cloves garlic, crushed and chopped
500ml white wine. I love using cooking wine but any dry white is
    good
200ml (7fl oz) double cream

Make sure your mussels are cleaned and get rid of any beards and barnacles. Discard any with broken shells.

Put the onions, garlic and butter in a heavy-based pot, big enough to take all your mussels, and sweat until the onions are soft. Add your white wine and leave to simmer for 5 minutes, then add your cream and stir. Now it's time for the mussels!

Add in all your mussels and put the lid of your pot on for them to steam through. You are looking for them all to open nicely, with the meat looking plump and ready to eat. I like to stir after 4 to 5 minutes, which also gives me a chance to check they are getting steamed evenly. When all of the shells are open, take off the heat and decant into bowls.

Serve with a crusty French stick and butter. Remember to leave a bowl in the centre of the table for the shells.

Scallops with Black Pudding and Garlic Butter

This is what I used to woo my boyfriend with most weekends. It's now my husband's all-time favourite (so it worked!).

Serves 4

4 slices of black pudding (take the plastic skin off)
16 scallops
2 tbsp olive oil
Garlic butter . . . the more the better but 150g (5oz) should do it. Go to Sides and Sauces (p. 94) to see how we make ours.

We pair this with a range of sides, sometimes salad and crusty bread, or crushed potatoes and spinach. Depending on what you are serving your scallops with, make sure that the prep for your sides is all done before you go on to the scallop and black pudding cooking, as these will need to be served immediately and they do not take long.

Put the black pudding under the grill for 5 minutes each side until cooked through. While the black pudding is grilling, rinse the scallop meat in cold water and place on some kitchen paper to dry fully. Put the scallops in the frying pan one at a time in a circle like the numbers on a clock and pan fry for 2 minutes each side, turning them over one after the other in a clockwise direction so they are cooked evenly. Turn off the heat, add the garlic butter to the pan and shake to coat all the scallops with the garlic butter ready to serve. Plate up on top of your slices of black pudding and sides.

Oysters with a Hot Garlic Butter

4–6 oysters per person
125g (4oz) salted butter at room temperature for each 6 oysters
4 cloves of garlic, crushed
Small bunch of parsley, finely chopped

Refer to page 33 to see how to shuck an oyster safely.
When all oysters are shucked, lay them on a baking tray,
oyster side up. You may find some tipping over and the
juice spilling out, but don't worry too much about that.

Make your garlic butter by putting the butter, garlic
and parsley in a small bowl and mixing with a fork until
all combined. Put dollops of the garlic butter on the
oysters and add a disc of garlic, about the size of a 50p
piece, and put under a preheated hot grill for 5-10
minutes or until the oysters have plumped up and the
butter is bubbling.

Be warned, these oyster shells will be very, very hot,
so please take care when serving. Serve with some nice
crusty bread.

Three-Cheese Baked Oysters

Serves 4 as a starter
20 oysters
200g (7oz) full fat cream cheese
100g (4oz) Isle of Mull cheddar, grated
200g (7oz) gruyère cheese, grated
1 tbsp cayenne pepper
2 cloves garlic, minced

Put all the ingredients except the oysters into a bowl and mix together.

Shuck your oysters as instructed on page 33, and lay them on a baking tray, oyster side up.

Preheat the oven to 200°C/400°F/gas 6.

Top each oyster with a teaspoon of the cheese mixture and bake in the oven for 10 minutes until the topping is golden.

Cod and Mull Cheddar Gratin

A perfect family dish. Serve with your choice of sides – I like chunky potato wedges and some buttery green beans.

Serves 4

3 tbsp butter
3 tbsp flour
500ml (17fl oz) full fat milk
200g (7oz) Isle of Mull cheddar or another strong cheddar, grated
2 tbsp mustard (I prefer Dijon)
20g (1oz) chives, chopped
Salt and pepper to taste
4 fillets of cod, boneless and skinless
200g (7oz) panko breadcrumbs
1 tbsp olive oil
200g (7oz) spinach, washed

Start by making your Mull cheddar sauce. Melt your butter on a low heat in a heavy-based saucepan, take off the heat and stir in the flour to make a roux. With the heat back on, slowly add the milk bit by bit and stir with a whisk until you get a smooth thick creamy sauce. Add half of the grated cheese, the mustard, half of the chives and a little salt and pepper to taste. Put the sauce to one side when you are happy with the seasoning.

Chop the cod up into cubes and put in the bottom of four individual gratin or other small oven-proof

dishes. My preferred dish is 20 × 12.5cm (8 × 5in). You can also make one large gratin dish if you would prefer to serve it family style. Bear in mind that if you are doing it in one dish you will need to amend cooking times and make them a bit longer, depending on the size of your dish.

Mix the panko breadcrumbs with the olive oil, the remaining cheddar and chives and put to one side.

Layer your gratin dishes first with spinach, then your sauce and finally top with your panko mix. Bake in the oven at 180°C/350°F/gas 4 for 25–35 minutes until golden brown on top and bubbling. If you are doing one large gratin dish, bake for 45 minutes to an hour. You can tell it's ready by checking that the fish in the middle has cooked white flesh.

Sides and Sauces

I think cooking and food has always been in my blood. Grandma, my dad's mum, was a minister's daughter and a traditional Scottish cook. She had owned her own restaurant and hotel. Her house is where I got my own inspiration as a cook. From a very young age you would find me in Grandma's back kitchen, spoon and bowl in hand. She taught me all about various ingredients and this was important in starting me off in the right direction.

Many of these simple ingredients can make wonderful sauces, butters and other additions to dishes that can make them delicious.

Chunky Tartare Sauce

A fish supper is a no go without it. And don't forget the mushy peas!

300g (10oz) mayonnaise
10 medium to large pickled gherkins, roughly chopped
4 tbsp capers, roughly chopped
Juice of ½ lemon
Generous pinch of salt and pepper

Mix all your ingredients together until combined. This will keep in the fridge in a jar for up to four weeks. I simply love this sauce with poached salmon, buttery new potatoes and spring greens.

Ridiculously Simple Seafood Sauce

Just a few short steps and you have a perfect emergency seafood sauce. Lobster, squat lobster, crab, prawns and hot-smoked salmon all go with it. Try it with seafood in a brioche roll.

300g (10oz) mayonnaise
3 tbsp Heinz Tomato Ketchup
3 tbsp Heinz Salad Cream (the secret)
Juice of ½ lemon
1 tbsp chives, chopped

Mix all the ingredients together, adding more tomato ketchup if you like a stronger flavour. I love this as a side with some freshly cooked langoustines and crusty bread with a thick layer of Scottish butter. Again, this will keep in a jar in the fridge for four weeks.

Sweet Chilli Mayo

This is so simple and works really well with Cajun hot-smoked salmon, but actually is perfect with any flavour of hot-smoked salmon.

200g (7oz) mayonnaise
200g (7oz) Blue Dragon Sweet Chilli Dipping Sauce

All you have to do is mix together! This also can be stored in the fridge for four weeks. So easy, and you would not believe how well this goes with hot-smoked salmon. Add this to hot-smoked salmon tacos or wraps to bring them to life with a jump start.

Flavoured Butters

Perfect with shellfish like langoustines and scallops, also lovely to serve with your bread if you are having a dinner party.

Garlic Butter

150g (5oz) salted butter, softened at room temperature
4 cloves garlic, crushed
Small bunch of parsley, finely chopped

Put the butter, garlic and parsley into a small bowl and mix with a fork until all combined.

Bacon and Basil Butter

150g (5oz) butter, softened at room temperature
4 rashers of smoked bacon, grilled well and left to cool
8 large basil leaves

Chop the bacon and the basil into small bits and mix with the butter.

You can also add other ingredients such as chopped dill and chive or chopped smoked trout and chive to the butter. These butters can all be frozen for up to five months. I like to put in ice cube trays and use when I need them.

Isle of Mull Cheddar Crouton

Perfect to top a creamy soup or as a light bite. I like to use sliced sourdough for this, but any good heavy bread will do.

---

2 large slices of bread
150g Isle of Mull cheddar, cut into slices

Put the bread under the grill for 3 to 5 minutes until golden brown on one side. Flip the toasted bread over and generously top with slices of cheddar. Put back under the grill until the cheese has melted and is bubbling. Cut in to bite-size chunks and serve with apple chutney or use to top your creamy Cullen (or Mull-en) Skink.

The Tobermory Fish Company and Shop
Baliscate Smokehouse,
Tobermory,
Isle of Mull,
Argyll,
PA75 6QA

Telephone: 01688 302120

Email: info@tobermoryfish.co.uk

Internet: www.tobermoryfish.co.uk

@tobermoryfishco

@tobermoryfishco